W9-BRY-640

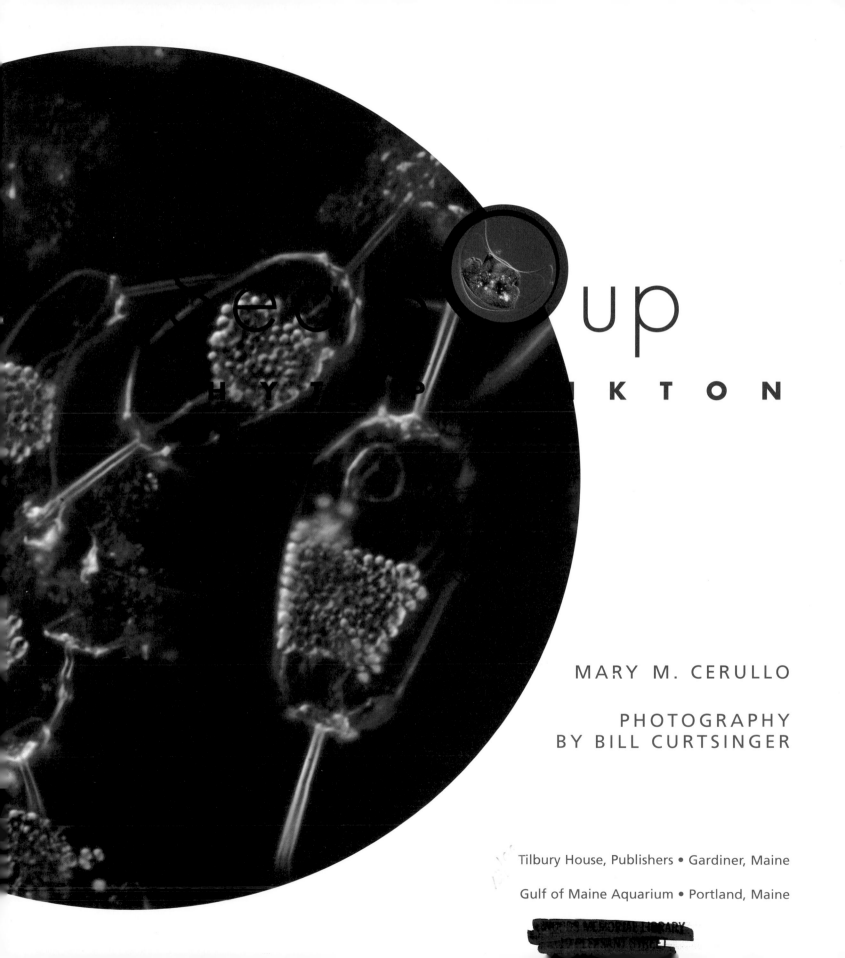

Sea Soup

PHYTOPLANKTON

MARY M. CERULLO

PHOTOGRAPHY
BY BILL CURTSINGER

Tilbury House, Publishers • Gardiner, Maine

Gulf of Maine Aquarium • Portland, Maine

SNIPES MEMORIAL LIBRARY
PLEASANT STREET

Imagine

that you are setting out on an undersea voyage to meet the most important creatures on earth. You step into your own personal submarine. A flick of a switch magically shrinks you and your ship smaller than the period at the end of this sentence. Because of your tiny size, the water around you flows by as thick as chowder. You look outside your porthole and come face-to-face with the strange, amazing life forms that are responsible for all other life in the sea—and for the oxygen we breathe and the atmosphere that surrounds the earth like a warm blanket.

These life forms are called phytoplankton (FIE-toe-plank-ton). They are tiny, microscopic plants, which is why they are also called microalgae. They don't look like the plants on land—they have no roots, stems, or leaves. Instead they resemble spiky balls, tiny harpoons, links on a bracelet, spaceships, and other shapes that defy description.

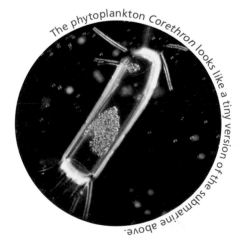

The phytoplankton Corethron looks like a tiny version of the submarine above.

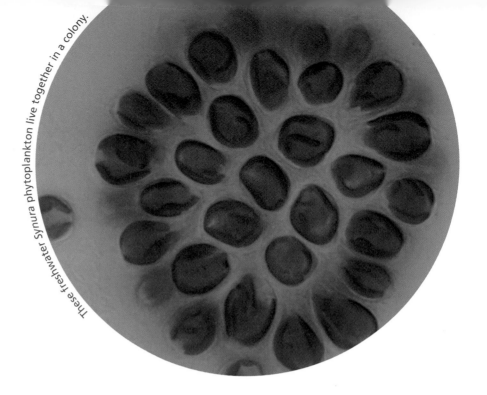

These freshwater Synura phytoplankton live together in a colony.

Phytoplankton need light in order to grow, so they are usually found near the surface of the water. Phytoplankton drift through the ocean on currents, waves, and tides. The word phytoplankton comes from the Greek words for "plant" and "floating." (Many tiny floating plants are called phytoplankton while one all by itself is a phytoplankter.) The first phytoplankton existed 3 billion years ago, when the earth was less than half as old as it is today. These microscopic plants helped create the ozone layer in the upper atmosphere that protects us from the harmful rays of the sun.

Phytoplankton are incredibly small. Each one is a single cell or a chain of identical cells. One teaspoon of sea water can hold a million phytoplankton. Most of the photos in this book were taken through a microscope that made the phytoplankton appear hundreds of times larger than they actually are.

There are thousands of different phytoplankton. Scientists are reluctant to guess how many kinds there are because new ones are being discovered all the time. A few years ago, after researchers built even more powerful microscopes, they discovered new kinds of phytoplankton that until then they had thought were just dust specks on their slides.

Phytoplankton don't just live at the surface of the ocean. They are also found on mud flats along the seashore and in freshwater ponds. If you collect a jar of pond water and keep it on the windowsill for a few days, the water will turn pea-soup green as the phytoplankton bloom in the sunlight.

But for now, let's continue our journey through sea soup

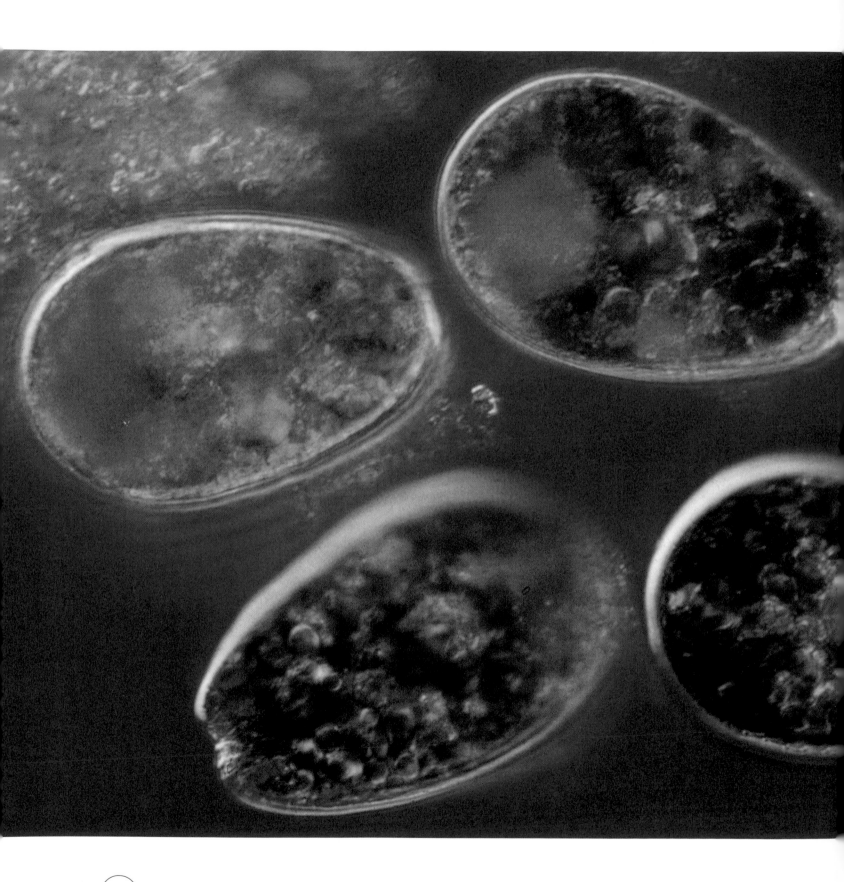

Are they plants or are they animals ?

Prorocentrum lima
Most phytoplankton float, but not this dinoflagellate. It latches onto seaweeds and floating logs to keep from sinking.

It's n⬤t always easy to tell.

Normally, plants make their own food from sunlight, and animals hunt and capture their food. But a visit to our microscopic world shows us, like Alice in Wonderland, that nothing is quite what it seems. Some phytoplankton behave like plants, some like animals, and some like both.

Phytoplankton live at the surface of the sea, or as far under the water as the sun's light can reach. If you dive deeper into the ocean in your miniature submarine, you will see that light fades quickly after the first 30 feet or so until it disappears completely by the time you sink to about 600 feet.

You can think of the thin layer of water at the surface of the ocean as "plankton soup." Here there is sunlight, water, and carbon dioxide for phytoplankton to make their own food. Mixed with nutrients like phosphorus and nitrogen (which are the same fertilizers we put on our gardens), phytoplankton can bloom in huge numbers. Sometimes these blooms become so thick they change the color of the water to red, green, or brown.

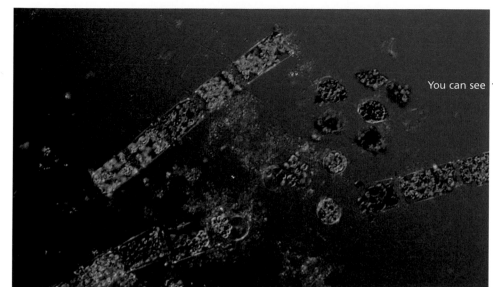

You can see the green chlorophyll inside this diatom *Guinardia*.

Phytoplankton and other plants have a chemical called chlorophyll (CLOR-o-fill) that captures the sunlight and changes it into food—sugars and starches—faster than the blink of an eye. This chemical reaction takes just a hundred-millionth of a minute and is called photosynthesis (foto-SIN-thi-sis). It also makes oxygen, which humans and other animals need to breathe.

All phytoplankton use sunlight to make their own food, but some also have other ways to survive. Some microalgae capture small animals or phytoplankton many times bigger than themselves. They spear them with their sharp harpoons and then siphon out their insides. Others farm little batches of bacteria that are attracted to the phytoplankton, like bees to honey, by the sugars that leak out from the microscopic plants. When there's not enough sunlight for photosynthesis, the phytoplankton eat the bacteria.

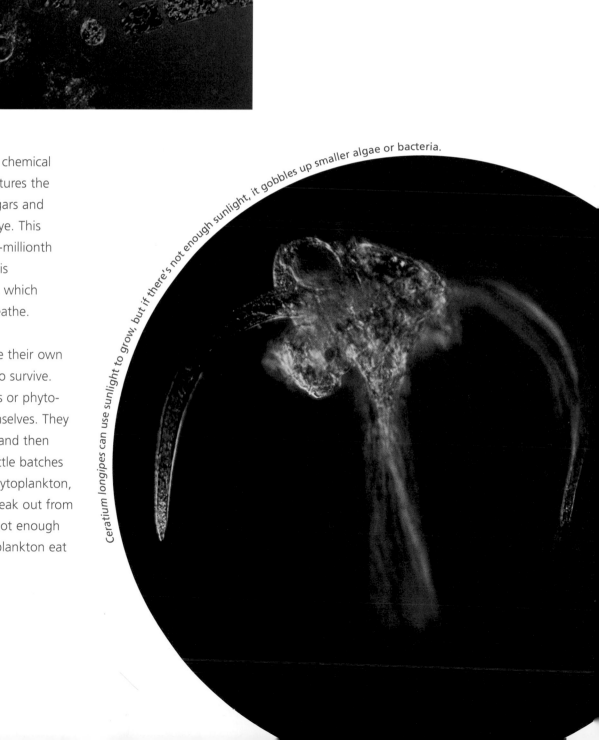

Ceratium longipes can use sunlight to grow, but if there's not enough sunlight, it gobbles up smaller algae or bacteria.

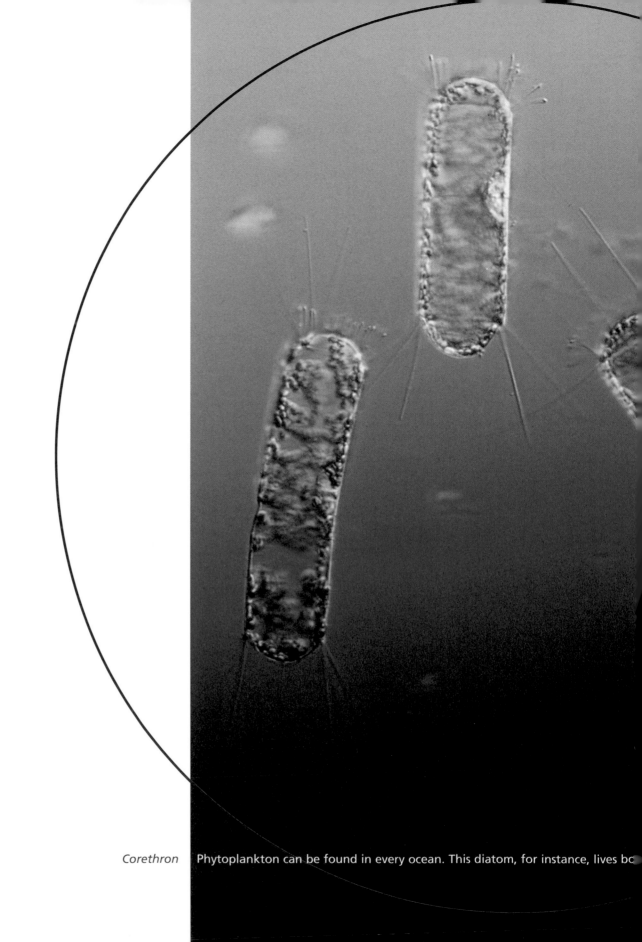

Corethron Phytoplankton can be found in every ocean. This diatom, for instance, lives bo

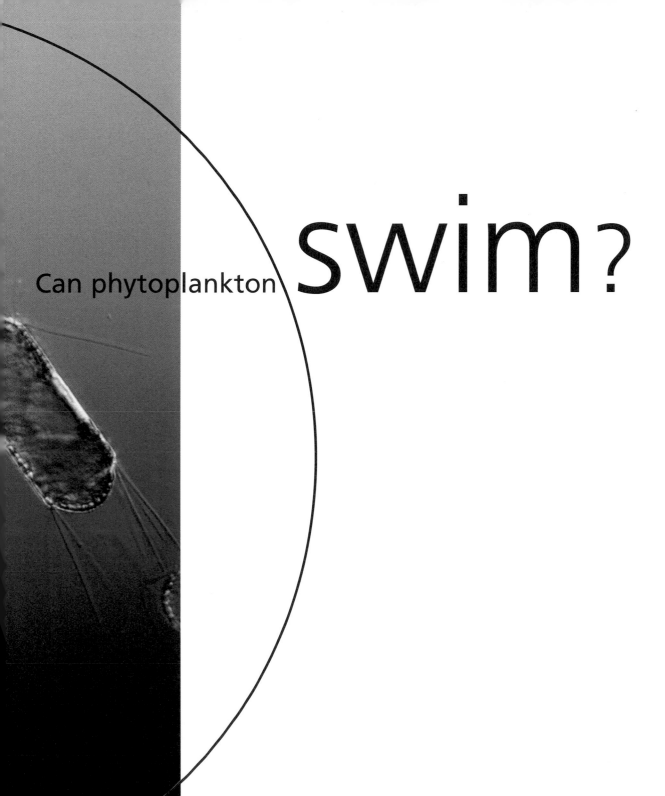

Can phytoplankton **swim?**

...n the Antarctic and in tropical seas, but it's not very common anywhere.

afloat.

Phytoplankton have lots of tricks for staying

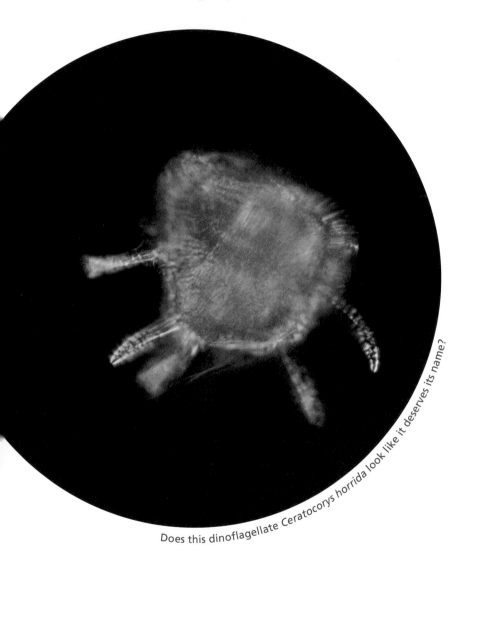

Does this dinoflagellate Ceratocorys horrida look like it deserves its name?

Most land plants are rooted in one place, while most animals can move. Although phytoplankton do drift with the waves and currents, many have little tails, called flagella (fla-JELL-a), that let them swim weakly from place to place. Dinoflagellates (dine-o-FLA-jell-ates) have two tails. One runs down the length of its body, and the other runs around its middle like a belt. They beat together, making the dinoflagellate twirl forward like a spinning top. These phytoplankton prefer calm water where they can gather at the surface and tread water or dive into deeper water to find nutrients.

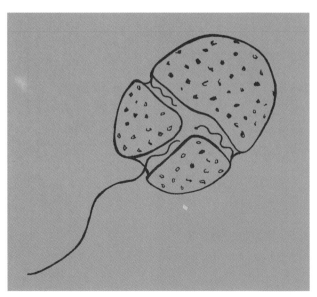

Dinoflagellate *Gymnopdinium*   Drawn by Bill Curtsinger.

10

Another type of phytoplankton is the diatom (DIE-a-tom), which looks like a plant inside its own little glass greenhouse. Diatoms are floaters. Their wild assortment of shapes help them to catch the currents, but their glass houses make them slightly heavier than seawater. To help them float, some store oil as extra food, because oil is lighter than water. Some have glass spines like waterwings; others form long chains, spirals, or circles that help keep them afloat like life preservers. Diatoms often live where waves and currents bump them back up toward the surface as they begin to sink.

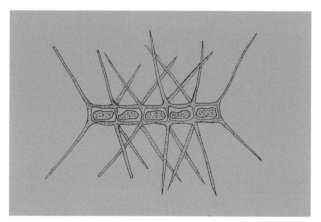

Diatom *Chaetoceros*   Drawn by Bill Curtsinger.

Phytoplankton, even ones with two tails, aren't great swimmers. But they can move very short distances, far enough to find a fresh supply of nutrients. It's a delicate balance between staying close to the light and sinking into a new bit of water where there is more nourishment.

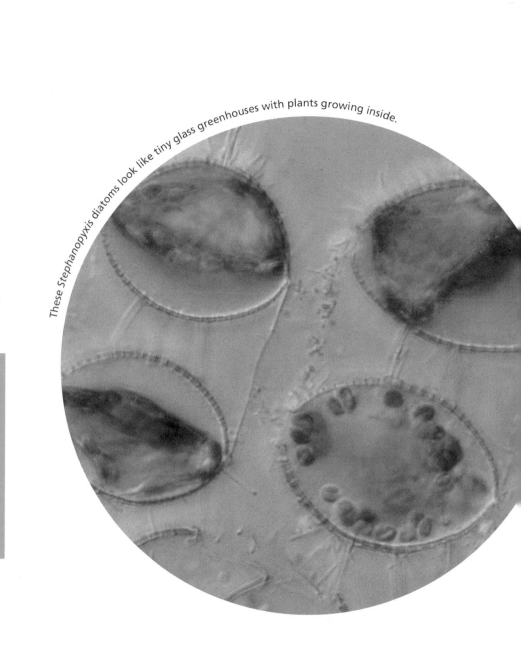

These *Stephanopyxis* diatoms look like tiny glass greenhouses with plants growing inside.

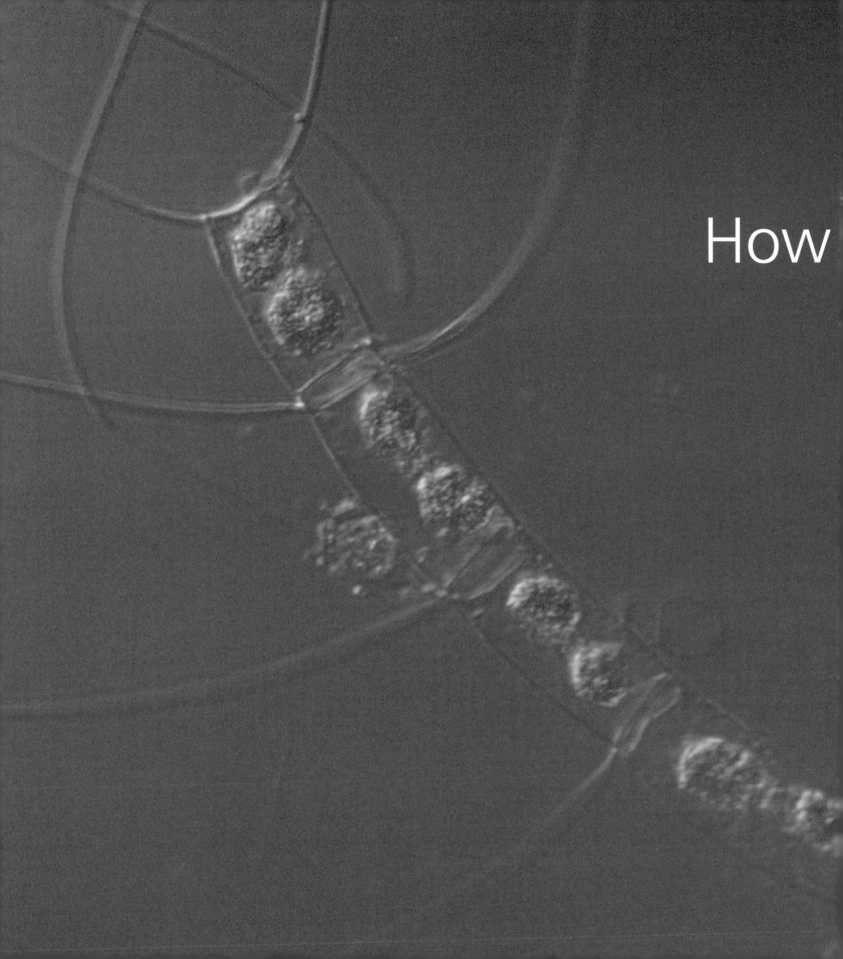

How

many phytoplankton does it take to fill a humpback whale?

Chaetoceros

These diatoms form long chains that help them float near the surface. Their spines, which also help them float, are sometimes as sharp as steak knives and can cut the delicate gills of fish.

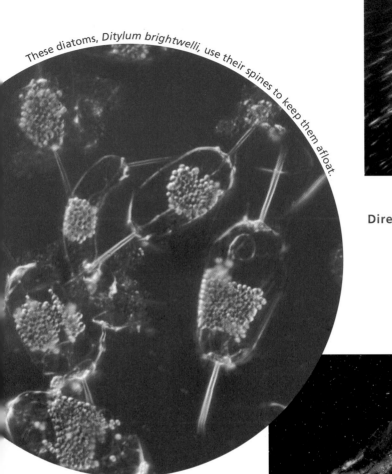

These diatoms, Ditylum brightwelli, *use their spines to keep them afloat.*

Directly or indirectly, phytoplankton feed everything else in the ocean,
even whales.

Tiny, floating animals called zooplankton (ZOE-o-plank-ton) eat the phytoplankton. Zooplankton, in turn, may be eaten by small fishes. These are eaten by bigger fishes on up the food chain to sharks, seabirds, and whales.

In order to feel full, a humpback whale may need to eat a ton of herring (about 5,000 fish). These herring have fed on zooplankton, such as shrimp-like creatures called krill (left), each of which has fed on as many as 130,000 diatoms. Therefore, one meal for a humpback may represent more than 400 billion diatoms!

This food chain of phytoplankton to zooplankton to fish to whale is fairly short, but in real life, diatoms feed many different kinds of animals. A food chain quickly branches into a food web, a more complex network of plants and animals in which one may become food for several others.

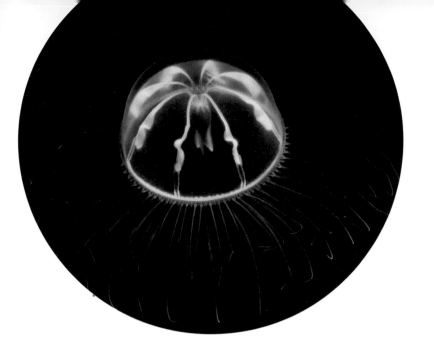

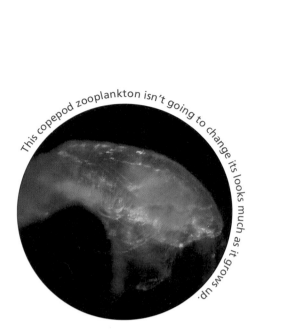

This copepod zooplankton isn't going to change its looks much as it grows up.

It's clear to see why many people call phytoplankton "the grass of the sea." Growing on the underside of the Antarctic ice is a lush, green pasture of diatoms which will, directly or indirectly, feed krill, penguins, squid, seals, sea lions, fishes, and whales.

Most zooplankton are microscopic, but some larger animals, such as the jellyfish above, also count as zooplankton because they drift along at the mercy of the wind and the waves. Some zooplankton, like the baby crab below, do not look anything like their parents. It will take many changes before they start to look like miniature adults. Other kinds of zooplankton stay the same all their lives.

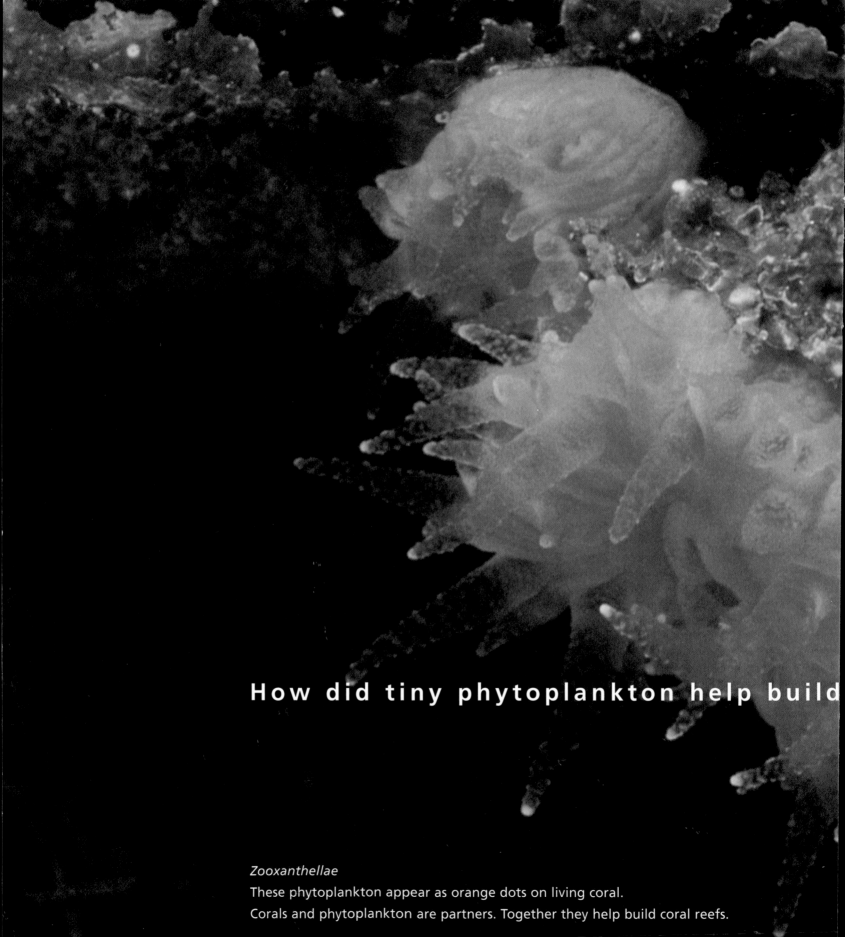

How did tiny phytoplankton help build

Zooxanthellae
These phytoplankton appear as orange dots on living coral.
Corals and phytoplankton are partners. Together they help build coral reefs.

the largest structures on earth **?**

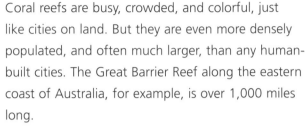

Coral reefs are busy, crowded, and colorful, just like cities on land. But they are even more densely populated, and often much larger, than any human-built cities. The Great Barrier Reef along the eastern coast of Australia, for example, is over 1,000 miles long.

Coral reefs are the result of a unique partnership between plants and animals—a type of phytoplankton called zooxanthellae (zoe-zan-THELL-ee) and small, vase-shaped animals called coral polyps (paul-UPS). The coral polyp takes calcium carbonate from the sea water to build itself a limestone house. Millions of these limestone houses create a coral reef. But the coral polyps couldn't build a reef without the help of their plant companions, the zooxanthellae. Zooxanthellae are dinoflagellates that live inside a thin layer of tissue linking all the coral polyps together. (You can think of it like having small plants growing under your skin.) Other animals, such as sponges and the giant *Tridacna* clam (left), often have phytoplankton living with them, too.

Besides providing food and oxygen to the polyp, the zooxanthellae help the coral take minerals from the sea water to build its limestone skeleton. They also give the corals their vibrant colors of pink, yellow, orange, purple, or red. If the water temperature gets too warm for them, the zooxanthellae leave or die, and the coral turns white like a skeleton.

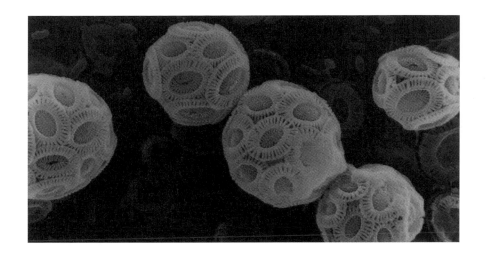

Another amazing builder is a phytoplankter called the coccolithophore (cock-o-LITH-o-for), a microscopic plant encased in many armored plates (top photo). As many as 1,500 plates could fit on the period at the end of this sentence. When billions of coccolithophores bloom at one time, astronauts in space can see the ocean's surface turn white (bottom photo).

After coccolithophores die, they sink to the bottom of the sea where they pile on top of each other until the weight of layer after layer of coccolithophores transforms them into rock. After millions of years, the coccolithophores, now transformed into limestone, are pushed up to the earth's surface to create towering structures like the White Cliffs of Dover in England—or small ones like a piece of chalk for your blackboard.

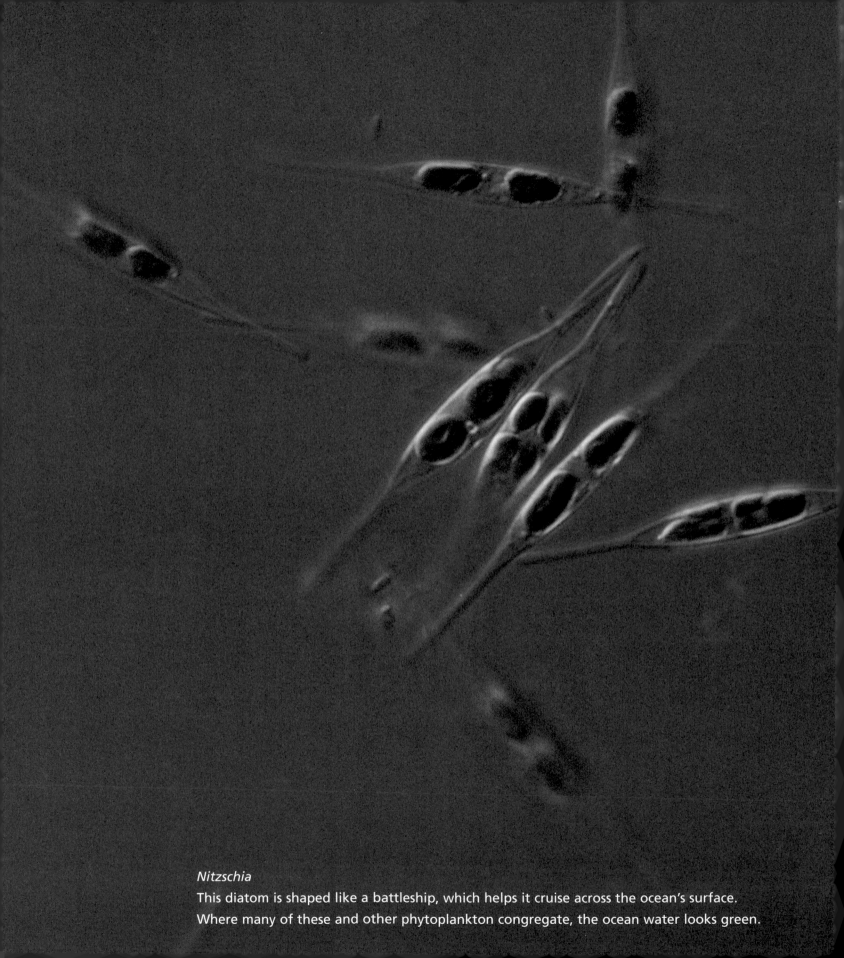

Nitzschia
This diatom is shaped like a battleship, which helps it cruise across the ocean's surface.
Where many of these and other phytoplankton congregate, the ocean water looks green.

Why is the ocean blue (or not) ?

Phytoplankton color the sea.

High above the deck of a fishing boat, a crew member is perched in the crow's nest scanning the sea surface for good places to fish. When he yells, "Green water!" the crew leaps into action, setting nets to haul in schools of fish.

Although the sea's surface is partly a reflection of the color of the sky, the ocean's color also depends on what is floating in it. Where there is phytoplankton, the ocean looks green. Where there is no plankton—and no food to feed schools of fishes—the water appears deep blue.

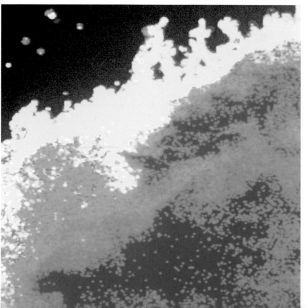

Satellites can see all the earth's oceans from 440 miles up in space. Their instruments measure the brightness of the water's surface. Water with a lot of phytoplankton reflects less light (the phytoplankton absorb the light) than areas without life, so satellite images show where phytoplankton live—near the coasts and in the colder regions of the open ocean, where nutrients from land help them thrive.

In the tropical seas where coral reefs occur, you might expect to see green water full of life, but instead, the water is so clear and blue you can see a hundred feet around you in any direction. But if you dive into cold ocean waters, you can see only a few inches ahead of you because the water is a salty soup of phytoplankton, zooplankton, and the nutrients they use.

Thanks to certain phytoplankton, the ocean sometimes glows at night. When these tiny plants are present, a ship leaves a shimmering wake behind it, or your footprints on the beach sparkle in the surf after you pass by. The light is from dinoflagellates that act like underwater fireflies, and create bioluminescence (buy-o-loom-in-ES-sense), the scientific word for cold, living light.

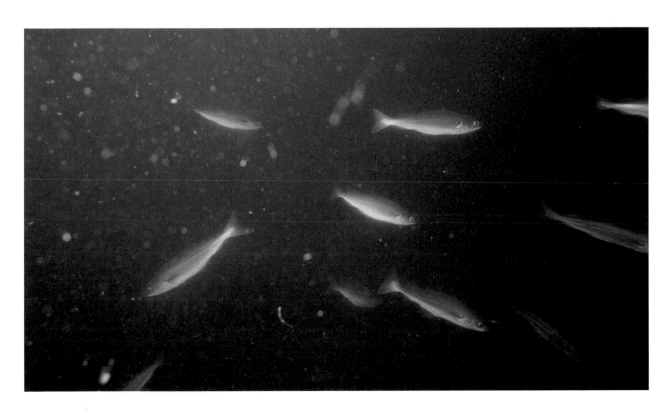

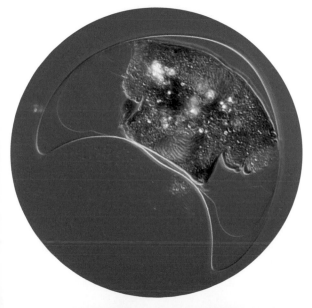

No one knows why some phytoplankton, like the one at the left, called *Pyrocystis lunula,* make their own "cold fire." Some people think it may be to startle animal plankton that feed on them, but other people ask, "Wouldn't it make them easier to be seen?" In any case, each single phytoplankton can bioluminesce only once every 24 hours—it takes a lot of energy to make underwater fireworks!

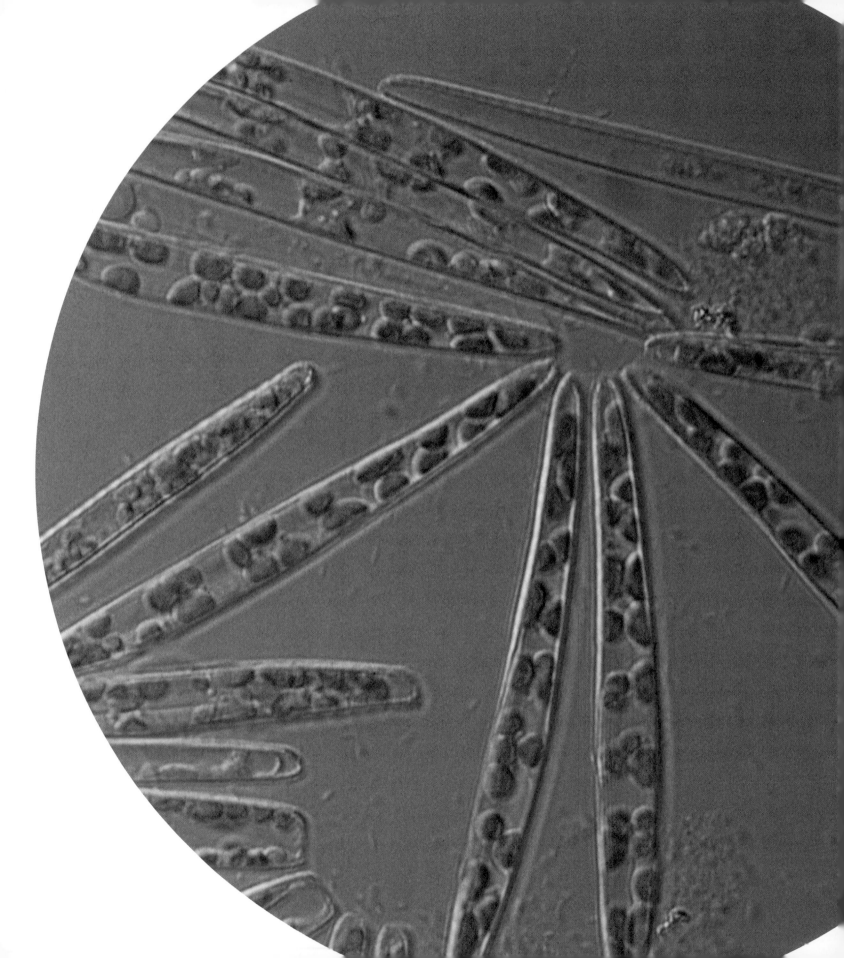

Are there *killer* phytoplankton ?

Pseudonitzschia

Even scientists sometimes have a hard time telling phytoplankton apart. But it's important not to mistake this poisonous diatom *Pseudonitzschia* for the harmless *Nitzschia* on page 20. This dangerous character can kill sea lions, pelicans, and dolphins, and cause permanent memory loss in humans who eat clams or mussels that have eaten it.

Beware the attack of deadly phytoplankton *!*

Prorocentrum lima won't kill you, but it may make you so sick you wish you were dead!

On a fall day in 1987, Torch, a large humpback whale, was leaping out of the water and slapping his tail fluke on the water, much to the delight of whale watchers off the coast of Cape Cod, Massachusetts. An hour and a half later, the huge, entertaining whale was dead. What could kill one of the biggest animals of the sea so quickly? Biologists examined his body and found that the mackerel that the whale had recently eaten contained poisonous dinoflagellates. The great whale had been killed by microscopic plants.

There are thousands of different kinds of phytoplankton, but only about 75 of those produce poisons called biotoxins. (Researchers call a poison made by a plant or an animal a biotoxin.) Some phytoplankton biotoxins are more poisonous than cobra venom, but the clams, oysters, or fish that eat them don't usually get sick. Instead, the toxins build up in their meat until they are so concentrated they can sicken or kill animals higher up the food chain, including salmon, sea lions, dolphins, manatees, whales, pelicans, and even humans.

When people eat the clams and oysters that ate the toxic phytoplankton, they may get sick. Some toxins cause a person to become numb and have a hard time breathing. Other kinds give you diarrhea. Still others make people lose their memory so they can't even remember their names.

No one knows why phytoplankton make biotoxins. It must take a lot of energy to cook up these poisonous brews, and no one can figure out what advantage this gives the phytoplankton. The biotoxins don't keep them from getting eaten or help them compete for space or nutrients.

If there are only a few toxic phytoplankton in the water, they don't create a problem. Some phytoplankton stay quiet inside little shells, like seeds, until conditions are right for them to bloom. Scientists are beginning to be able to predict what conditions favor the sudden bloom of toxic phytoplankton. They may break out of their shells (called cysts) and begin to grow like crazy after a heavy rain, a flood of nutrients, or a string of sunny days. The phytoplankton grow so thick that they sometimes turn the water red, brown, or even green. When this occurs, people call it a "red tide" (even if the water isn't red). Scientists call it a HAB, for Harmful Algal Bloom.

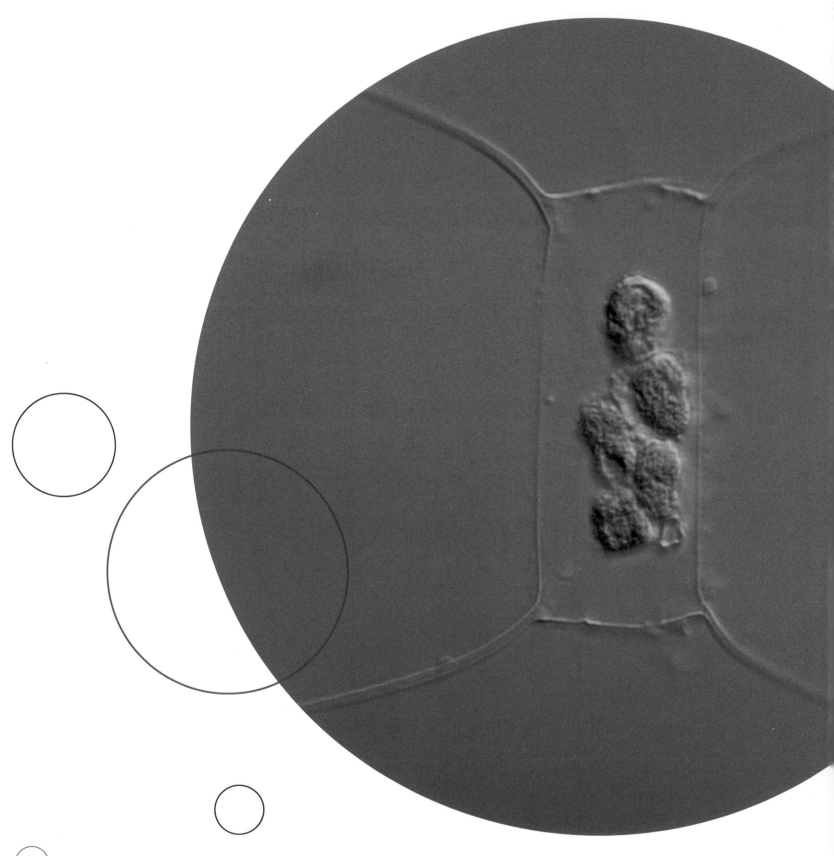

Have you *thanked* a phytoplankter today **?**

Chaetoceros

Try to imagine how many tiny diatoms it must take to create oil, diatomaceous earth, and other products humans use.

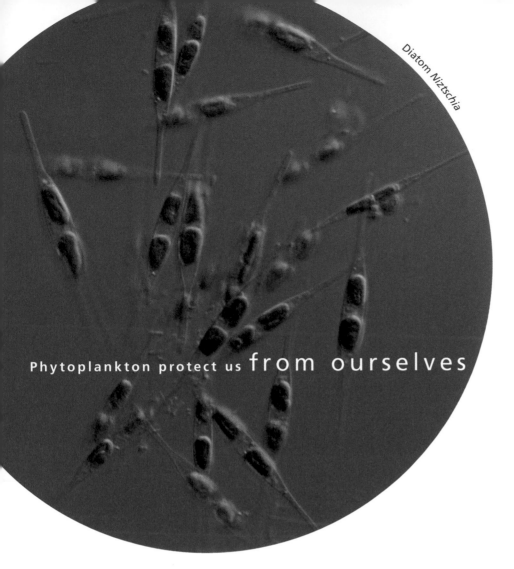

Diatom *Niztschia*

Phytoplankton protect us from ourselves

ozone layer. (Chemicals we use in some hair sprays and refrigerators make the ozone layer thinner.) The ozone layer helps protect us from the harmful UV (ultraviolet) rays of the sun that can cause sunburn and even skin cancer.

Many of us heat our homes with the remains of ancient phytoplankton. When they died, the phytoplankton sank to the ocean floor and were eventually buried under layers of mud, sometimes thousands of feet thick. They changed into oil deposits over millions of years. Eventually, geologists drilled into the ocean floor and brought the phytoplankton, now changed into oil or natural gas, back to the surface of the sea. Most oil deposits are found under the ocean or under land that once was covered by the sea.

The earth has been getting warmer over the last 100 years, and many people blame it on the "greenhouse effect." They believe that the burning of fossil fuels and rain forests releases extra carbon-dioxide into the air. This traps heat in the upper atmosphere, causing global warming. Each year, phytoplankton take nearly half the carbon dioxide we release by burning coal, oil, and gas and turn it into shells and other body parts. When the phyto-plankton die or are eaten, some of the carbon inside them sinks harmlessly to the bottom of the sea. Phytoplankton use 3 billion tons of carbon dioxide each year, slowing down the warming of the earth. Phytoplankton also help replace the

In recent years people have added to what the sea can provide through aquaculture—raising fish, shellfish, and other foods from the sea in shallow bays. Some phytoplankton are grown especially to feed animals being raised in aquaculture operations. Products made from phytoplankton also filter swimming pools, distill fruit juice, wine, and beer, put the polish in toothpaste, and keep dynamite from exploding too soon. Perhaps most important, phytoplankton help us to breathe. About half of the world's oxygen comes from phytoplankton. That means every other breath you take is thanks to phytoplankton.

How

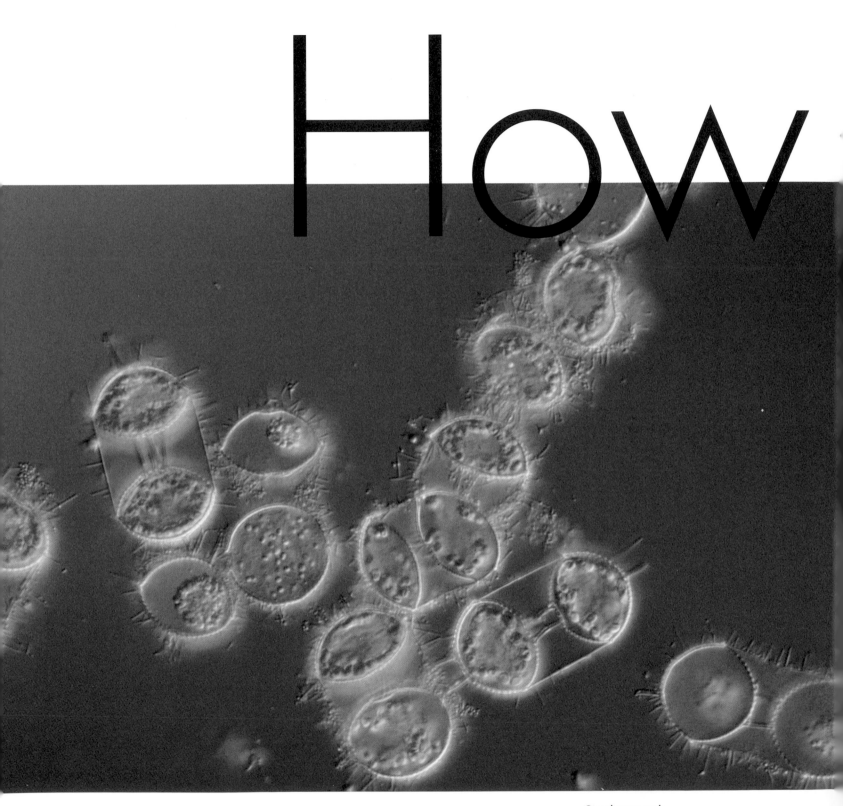

Stephanopyxis

When you shine blue light on phytoplankton

do we know so much about things most of us have never seen **?**

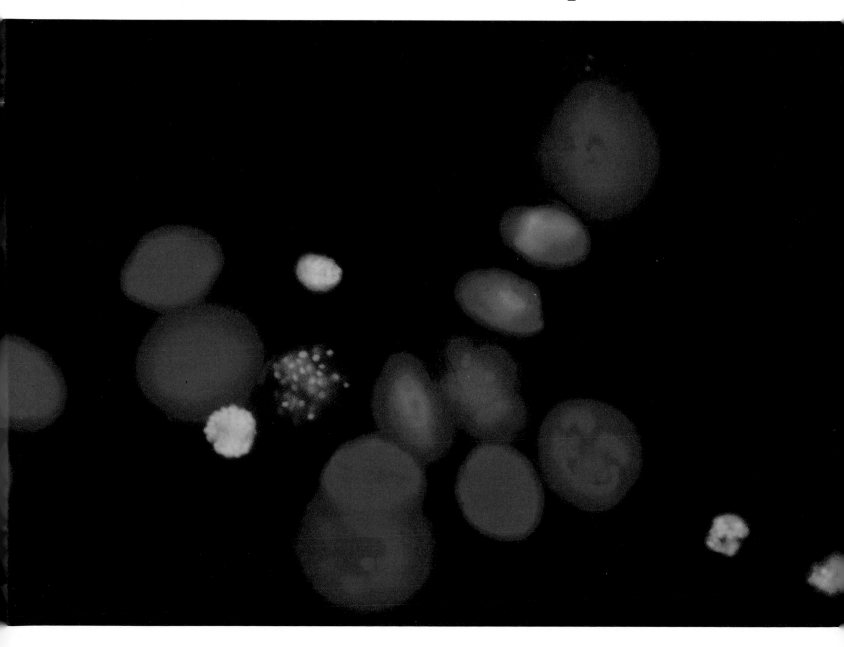

he chlorophyll inside the plant reflects back red.

Scientists study phytoplankton from up close to very far away.

Scientists have many tools to help them learn about phytoplankton. Microscopes are our best tools for studying tiny plants that are one thousand times smaller than the thickness of a blade of grass. Scientists use regular microscopes that can make phytoplankton appear 1,000 times larger than their actual size, electron microscopes that magnify them 1,000,000 times, and fluorescent microscopes that use blue light to make phytoplankton glow. Another type of microscope—a flow cytometer—measures and counts thousands of phytoplankton each minute as a narrow stream of water flows past an electronic camera. Satellites hundreds of miles above the ocean's surface can track the blooms of phytoplankton from season to season to help scientists predict where this abundant food supply will nurture the growth of all marine animals.

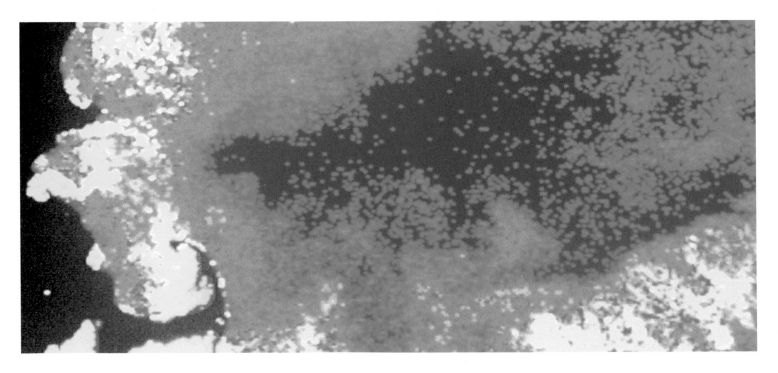

Sometimes we learn about phytoplankton from noticing changes in the environment. A change in the water color, dolphins beaching themselves, or pelicans acting strangely are clues that there may be a bloom of toxic phytoplankton. Volunteer scientists then catch phytoplankton using fine-mesh plankton nets. They examine the water with field microscopes to look for harmful phytoplankton. Even young students can help collect and identify the samples. Scientists follow up with laboratory tests and if toxic phytoplankton are found, they warn people not to dig for clams and other shellfish until the "red tide" event has passed.

There is even a phytoplankton ZOO!

Bigelow Laboratory for Ocean Sciences sits at the edge of a huge vat of phytoplankton called the Atlantic Ocean. Here along the coast of Maine, more than 40 scientists study phytoplankton, using the tools we described. Many of the scientists go to sea for weeks at a time studying phytoplankton. Scientists who stay on shore grow individual types of phytoplankton in test tubes. These "cultures" of the same kind of phytoplankton allow researchers to learn more about individual species. But, like raising rare and exotic plants, culturing phytoplankton is sometimes very hard to do. The scientists at Bigelow Laboratory have been able to raise more than 1,700 different kinds of phytoplankton. Their microscopic "zoo" is the world's largest collection of phytoplankton.

Many of the phytoplankton at Bigelow Laboratory are used by other researchers around the world to develop new foods or medicines or to feed animals raised in aquaculture operations. About 50 different types of phytoplankton are supplied to sea farmers by Bigelow Laboratory to feed oysters, clams, mussels, and other plankton-eaters.

Scientists are also looking for how phytoplankton can help us learn more about the ocean and how to take care of it. They are asking questions like, Why do some phytoplankton turn bad? What do phytoplankton need to survive?

They are also looking for better answers to many of the questions we have just explored. Who will find new answers? Who will come up with new questions? Maybe it will be you!

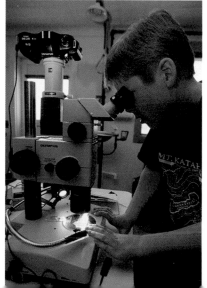

What's in a name ?

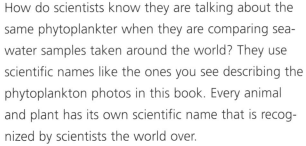

How do scientists know they are talking about the same phytoplankter when they are comparing seawater samples taken around the world? They use scientific names like the ones you see describing the phytoplankton photos in this book. Every animal and plant has its own scientific name that is recognized by scientists the world over.

Each plant or animal gets a Genus name (which is capitalized) and a species name (which is not). Both names are underlined or written in italics. This naming system was invented back in the 1750s by a Swedish scientist named Karl von Linné (who used the Latin version of his name, *Carolus Linnaeus*). Often these names describe some fact about the creature, such as its size, color, or even the person who first discovered it. *Pyrocystis lunula* (left) means "fire cell" and "moon," which describes the fact that this bioluminescent dinoflagellate, shaped like a crescent moon, glows like fire at night.

Usually an animal or plant has both a scientific name and a common name. For example, both *Charadon carcharias* and great white shark are names for a famous ocean hunter. But there are so many different kinds of phytoplankton that they usually have only scientific names, such as *Ceratium pentagonum* (which is a five-sided dinoflagellate).

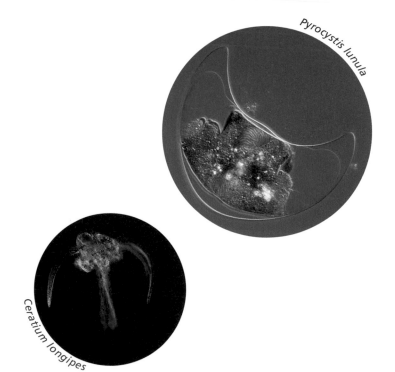

Pyrocystis lunula

Ceratium longipes

GLOSSARY

aquaculture	raising fish, clams, seaweed, and other foods from the sea in "sea farms"	page 31, 37
bioluminescence	the production of light by living things	23
biotoxin	a poison made by a plant or animal	27
bloom	the rapid growth of phytoplankton, often as a result of an increase in light or nutrients	6, 19, 34–35
coccolithophore	a tiny phytoplankter covered by 12 calcareous plates	19, 30
cyst	a protective shell that some phytoplankton make to survive harsh conditions	27
diatoms	phytoplankton with glass shells made of silica	11–15, 20–21, 24–25, 28–30
dinoflagellates	phytoplankton that often have two flagella	4–5, 10
food chain	a sequence of plants and animals in a community in which one member feeds on the member below it	14
food web	a complex interrelationship of who eats whom	14
fossil fuels	fuels that were created by the fossilization of plants or animals; includes oil, coal, and natural gas	30
global warming	the theory that carbon dioxide and other gases produced by burning fossil fuels are trapped in the upper atmosphere, absorbing and reflecting heat back to earth	30
microalgae	another word for phytoplankton	2, 7
nutrients	substances that promote growth and development	6, 27
phytoplankton	one-celled, microscopic, drifting plants	
red tide	a sudden bloom of poisonous phytoplankton	26–27, 35
toxic	poisonous	27, 35
zooplankton	plankton that are tiny floating animals	14–15
zooxanthellae	a group of phytoplankton that live in corals, some sea anemones, and *Tridacna* clams	16–19

RELATED READING

Baldwin, Robert. *This Is the Sea that Feeds Us.* Nevada City, CA: Dawn Publications, 1998.

Kovacs, Deborah and Kate Madin. *Beneath Blue Waters: Meetings with Remarkable Sea Creatures.* New York: Viking, 1996.

Epstein, Sam and Beryl Epstein. *What's For Lunch? The Eating Habits of Seashore Creatures.* New York: Macmillan Children's Books, 1985.

Tilbury House, Publishers
2 Mechanic Street • Gardiner, Maine 04345
800-582-1899 • http://www.tilburyhouse.com

Gulf of Maine Aquarium
P.O. Box 7549 • Portland, Maine 04112
207-772-2321 • http://octopus.gma.org

Text copyright © 1999 Mary M. Cerullo.
Photographs and drawings copyright © 1999 Bill Curtsinger.
Photos on pages 22 and 34 (lower) courtesy of Bigelow Laboratory.

First printing: November 1999.   10 9 8 7 6 5 4 3 2 1

All rights reserved. No part of this publication may be reproduced or
transmitted in any form or by any means, electronic or mechanical, including photocopy,
recording, or any information storage or retrieval system, without permission in writing from the publisher.

• This book is dedicated to Alan Lishness, who has a true gift for discovering possibilities and partnerships.

• Our thanks to Robert Anderson, Maureen Keller, Louis Sage, and Julie Sexton of Bigelow Laboratory, Bigelow board members Chris
Flower and Neil Rolde, Hans Kusters and Michael Hallacy of Zeiss Optical Systems, Bill Douthitt, Charles Gregory of Southern Maine
Technical College, Georgi Thompson and her class, and Owen Curtsinger. Thanks to Maureen Keller, Charles Gregory, and Betsy
Stevens for reviewing the manuscript. Any errors that remain are the author's, not theirs!

Library of Congress Cataloging-in-Publication Data
Cerullo, Mary M.
Sea soup : phytoplankton / Mary M. Cerullo ; photography by Bill Curtsinger.
p. cm   Includes bibliographical references (p.).
Summary: Discusses the microscopic organisms known as phytoplankton and the important functions they serve in replenishing earth's
atmosphere, in the marine food chain, and more.
ISBN 0-88448-208-1 (alk. paper)
1. Phytoplankton Juvenile literature. [1. Phytoplankton. 2. Plankton.] I. Curtsinger, Bill, 1946–   ill. II. Title. III. Title: Phytoplankton.
QK933.c47 1999   99-39210
579.8'1776—dc21   CIP

Design and layout: Geraldine Millham, Westport, MA • Editing and production: Jennifer Elliott, Barbara Diamond
Color scans and film: Integrated Composition Systems, Spokane, WA • Printing and binding: Worzalla Publishing, Stevens Point, WI

Sea S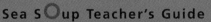up Teacher's Guide
Discovering the Watery World of Phytoplankton and Zooplankton
by Betsy T. Stevens, illustrated by Rosemary Giebfried

Paperback, $9.95   96 pages, illustrations
ISBN 0-88448-209-X   Children/Science Grades 3–7

The interesting and fun activities in Betsy Stevens' *Sea Soup Teacher's Guide* meet the challenge of
relating tiny, microscopic organisms to the lives of children. Discover and explore answers to some
strange questions. What is the recipe for Sea Soup? Are those tiny critters plants or animals, or maybe
something else? Why do they look more like creatures from outer space than the organisms we know
on land? What do giant clams, corals, whales, penguins, and humans have in common? How does the
Sea Soup grow? What if it stops growing?

   The inquiry-based activities range from designing and making a phytoplankter and collecting
phytoplankton to designing an experiment for exploring what factors influence the growth of phytoplankton and zooplankton. The emphasis is on science, but where appropriate math, geography,
language arts, and art are included. Each unit includes background information, objectives, a statement
of how it addresses the National Science Education Standards, materials, procedures, references, and
suggested websites.